BECAUSE I'M FAT

Understanding & Embracing Health Beyond Size

OLOJO CHRISTIANA

ISBN: 9798302738400

INTRODUCTION

Body image, as dictated by societal standards and media portrayals, has made the conversation about health and wellness quite convoluted. Weight, size, and health are often talked about in an oversimplified narrative that leads to misconceptions and stigmas damaging to individuals of all shapes and sizes. This book, **"BECAUSE AM FAT:** *Understanding & Embracing Health Beyond Size"* challenges such stories in the pursuit of more nuanced ways of thinking about health aside from mere numbers on the scale.

The journey of understanding that health extends beyond size is not only personal but also a social imperative. It is important to understand that health is multi-dimensional and runs on the dimensions of physical, mental, and emotional feelings that significantly vary from one individual to another as we go through a culture where the size of a person is associated with health and worth. The following book intends to shed light on the many experiences that cannot fit into one conventional mold of health but rather celebrates the diversity of bodies.

You will take a journey through personal stories and testimonials from people who struggled with their body image, health, and self-acceptance. These are powerful reminders that we each have different journeys. Sharing in the struggles, triumphs, and lessons learned with each, they create an experience with which the reader can most easily relate. It is in sharing these experiences that we hope to offer a sense of community and support for readers by embracing their journeys of health and self-acceptance. One of the aims of this book is to push against some very entrenched social norms with regard to perceptions about health and body image.

We will touch on the roles that diet culture, media portrayal, and societal expectations play in influencing our perceptions of health. By applying critical analysis, we learn how to take apart unhelpful stereotypes that foster body shaming and discrimination. This book is a call to action for a kinder approach to health: one that values the life of every person, regardless of their size.

In the subsequent chapters, we are going to look in more detail at nutrition, physical activity, mental well-being, and community support as some of the key aspects of health. There are so many benefits to the development of a health model that focuses on well-being instead of weight. An important focus will be on intuitive eating and joy of movement coupled with mental health. This comprehensive exploration sets out to equip the reader with knowledge and tools to forge a healthier relationship with their body and themselves.

As you wade through the pages of this book, we invite you to approach this with an open mind and heart. Be it to improve your own health, to support a loved one, or simply to be informed about the many nuances of body image and wellness, there's something for everyone. We invite you to reflect on your own experiences, question your assumptions, and begin to embrace that health is not one-size-fits-all.

"BECAUSE AM FAT: *Understanding & Embracing Health Beyond Size"* is more than a book; it's a movement toward the acceptance and compassionate understanding of health. We can co-create something new: redefine what health is for us, celebrate body diversity, and encourage people to uniquely own their journey. Let's begin on this transformative path, so that a sense of self-acceptance, understanding, and self-love for oneself and others will grow in our environment.

CONTENTS

INTRODUCTION

ACKNOWLEDGMENTS

CHAPTER 1: --REDEFINING HEALTH

CHAPTER 2: --------------------------------THE SCIENCE OF BODY DIVERSITY

CHAPTER 3: ----------------------------------NUTRITION: FUELING YOUR BODY

CHAPTER 4: -------------------------------------MOVEMENT FOR JOY, NOT PUNISHMENT

CHAPTER 5: --MENTAL HEALTH MATTERS

CHAPTER 6: ---THE ROLE OF COMMUNITY AND SUPPORT

CHAPTER 7: --NAVIGATING DIET CULTURE

CHAPTER 8: -------------------------------------PERSONAL STORIES OF TRANSFORMATION

CHAPTER 9: --------------------ADVOCATING FOR INCLUSIVITY IN WELLNESS

CHAPTER 10: --UNDERSTANDING EMOTIONAL EATING

CHAPTER 11: ------------------------THE IMPACT OF MEDIA AND SOCIETY

CHAPTER 12: ------------------SETTING REALISTIC GOALS FOR HEALTH

CHAPTER 13: ------------------------------------BUILDING HEALTHY RELATIONSHIPS WITH FOOD

CHAPTER 14: --------------------------CREATING A SUSTAINABLE HEALTH JOURNEY

READERS REVIEW

ABOUT THE AUTHOR

ACKNOWLEDGMENTS

I would like to extend my most sincere gratitude to all those who have made the writing of this book, " **BECAUSE AM FAT**: *Understanding & Embracing Health Beyond Size*.", a reality.

I would like to begin with the brave individuals who contributed their stories and experiences to this work. Your openness and vulnerability really brought depth to this work and provided insight that was invaluable in the myriad journeys of health and acceptance.

To my family and friends, thanks for the support and encouragement. Your belief in me has been a constant source of motivation, and I am grateful for your patience during the writing process.

I would like to give thanks to the health and wellness professionals whose research and expertise helped guide me on body positivity and holistic health. Your commitment to cultivating inclusivity and compassion in the field has inspired me to pick up the baton in fighting for a more accepting point of view on health.

Last but not least, to my readers: Thanks for taking this journey with me. I hope this resonates with you and empowers you to forge a different path to health and well-being for yourself. Let us rise together, rejoicing in body diversity in redefining what it will mean for us to be healthy.

Appreciative,

Olojo Christiana.

CHAPTER 1
REDEFINING HEALTH

As we live in a society that seems to still equate health with weight, now is a great time for us to step back and truly redefine what health really is. This chapter explores the ideas of health apart from weight but rather centers on the generally holistic approach: the physical, mental, and emotional well-being of a person. Incorporating a broader sense of understanding about health, one cultivates an all-encompassing nurturing mindset that focuses on body diversity and overall well-being.

WHAT DOES HEALTH MEAN BEYOND WEIGHT?

Traditionally, health has been measured by a number-a number on the scale. These narrow definitions provide ways of harmful stereotypes and stigmatizations to any persons who happen not to fit societal standards of weight and body size. However, health is a multidimensional construct that cannot be reduced to a single metric.

The Limitations of Weight as a Measure of Health

Weight alone does not explain health. A reason for a person's overall well-being may be genetic, life course, mental health, and social determinant-related reasons for health, such as healthcare access, nutrition, and community support. For example, a person could be heavier in weight yet be very active, eat right, and be mentally healthy. On the other hand, a person with a low body weight may be suffering from chronic stress, malnutrition, or a sedentary lifestyle.

Diverse Bodies

It is important to realize that health comes in many body shapes and sizes to enhance the acceptance of diversity regarding wellness. Body diversity, like any other human attribute, is a natural part of human existence, and each one has a unique set of circumstances that determines his or her health. By embracing this diverse nature, we will fail to support the injurious idea that people with only certain body types should be healthy and happy.

The Role of Self-Acceptance

Self-acceptance plays a core role in health redefinition. The ways in which individuals learn to accept and appreciate their bodies as they are will serve as a greater motivation to engage in self-care methods that respect personal values and life goals. Such a self-concept builds self-accepting attitudes, which invite them to orient themselves toward function instead of form; this will put them in contact with themselves in a less negative way, especially regarding body image.

THE IMPORTANCE OF HOLISTIC HEALTH

Holistic health considers the wholeness of a person-body, mind, and spirit-rather than isolating parts of health. It is a necessary comprehensive perspective to understand and promote well-being beyond size and weight.

Physical Health

Physical health includes proper nutrition, exercise, rest, and health care. A holistic approach invites a person to engage in activities that will maintain and promote physical well-being: eating for nourishment, moving the body regularly, resting, and having good medical care. And more importantly, it is not about diets and punishing workouts; rather, it's finding pleasure in movement and feeding the body with foods that feel good.

Mental and Emotional Health

Mental and emotional well-being is just as important to holistic well-being. Indeed, stress, anxiety, and depression surely have strong bearings on physical health; hence, these aspects of well-being should not be left unattended. Mindfulness, therapy, and self-care are some of the ways to develop a positive-oriented mindset and build resilience in the midst of life's ups and downs. In setting a good foundation of overall wellness, one must not forget mental health.

Social Connections and Community Support

People are naturally social animals, and health is deeply influenced by all connections with others. The integral approach to health also sees supportive community, relationships, and friendships as a necessary component to health. Having supportive friends and family, being connected into social networks, can build an even firmer sense of belonging; improved mental health will come too. Besides the above-mentioned significant aspects, the social factors that determine health are known as access to health care, education, and economic opportunities.

Holistic Integrations

The person may attempt to apply various practices in daily living that would contribute to the sense of holistic health, such as:

- Mindful Eating: Being more fully present with the act of eating; listening to body signals that indicate hunger; consuming foods for nourishment and joy.

- *Joyful Movement*: Engaging in forms of movement because it is enjoyable for an individual: dancing, hiking, yoga, or other activity that brings delight and comfort to the person.

- *Mindfulness Practices:* This may be through mindfulness, meditation, or journaling in order to increase emotional wellness and decrease stress. Building Community: Building supportive relationships and participating in community activities that create connection and a sense of belonging.

Redefining health is a shift in perspective-one that moves beyond weight and embraces a holistic understanding of well-being. By acknowledging the complexity of health and the different life journeys each human embarks on, we can consequently leave room for an inclusive, compassionate concept of wellness to arise. As we work to care for and love ourselves and one another, let us promote a body, health, and celebrate our diversity that makes humanity human. Let us not forget, as we journey through, that health is not a place of arrival but, rather, a lifelong journey into growth, acceptance, and self-love.

CHAPTER 2
THE SCIENCE OF BODY DIVERSITY

As we go deep into the health beyond size, there creates a need to understand the scientific reasoning behind body diversity. This chapter debates various kinds of body shapes and forms and how our body structure is influenced by genetics. We will discuss some myths about weight and health and get educated on how these things add to our overall health.

THE BODY TYPE AND GENETICS

Bodies come in a wide array of shapes and sizes due to an interacting web of genetics, environment, and lifestyle. It is important to learn about body types and the genes that influence them to better appreciate the diversity in human form.

The Role of Genetics

It is important to note that the body type of an individual can be determined by his or her height, structure of the bones, accumulation of fat, and even muscular tissue. Genetics plays a big role in accounting for the major part of body weight and composition among all individuals. To illustrate, some people are genetically predisposed to gain fat around certain areas, while some build muscle mass in no time.

Body Types: Ectomorph, Mesomorph, and Endomorph

While each of us is different, body types can be generally classified into three major categories: ectomorph, mesomorph, and endomorph.

- *Ectomorphs*: This usually have a lean body composition, narrow shoulders and hips, and a high metabolism. They may find it hard to gain weight or muscle mass.

-*Mesomorphs:* They are naturally more muscular, athletic, with broad shoulders; naturally, a high percentage of muscle mass is carried on their body frame. They gain weight or lose it rather sooner compared to other body types.

-*Endomorphs*: They have rounder bodies and are generally more disposed toward storing fat. While they struggle most with weight loss, building muscle for them is considered relatively easy.

These categories are, however, not set in stone, as many individuals may show characteristics of more than one body type. In addition, body types may change throughout one's lifetime based on factors related to aging, hormonal changes, and lifestyle.

The Influence of Environment and Lifestyle

Genetics forms the base, but the environmental factor and our ways of living contribute a great deal in setting our body type. The nutritional factors, physical activities, levels of stress, and sleeping habits have influences on body composition and general health. It would also be at this point that understanding such interaction will lead individuals to an improved appreciation of their body type and to make healthy choices.

DEBUNKING MYTHS ABOUT WEIGHT AND HEALTH

Despite the growing body of research that supports the notion of body diversity, a number of myths about weight and health endure.

These contribute to stigma and prevent people from accepting their bodies. We now discuss some of the most common myths related to weight and health.

Myth 1: Weight Equals Health

Perhaps the most insidious myth is the one that has to do with equating weight to health. Though weight may be suggestive of health, it certainly is not a direct indicator of the same. Many people with larger body weights can be metabolically fit and showcase normal levels of blood pressure, cholesterol, and sugar levels in their blood. Conversely, many people of smaller body weights can fall foul of health conditions emanating from insufficient nutrition or even a sedentary lifestyle - including a wide array of mental health disorders.

Myth 2: The Only Path to Better Health Is Losing Weight

Another inalienable truth is the belief that better health could only be achieved through losing weight. This can lead to a poor approach to diets and focus on quick fixes rather than long-term health benefits. As a matter of fact, it is possible to improve nutrition, increase physical activity, and attend to one's mental health, achieving great health benefits with or without weight change.

Myth 3: All Fat is Bad

The idea that all fat is bad for health is a myth. In reality, our bodies need healthy fats to perform several functions, such as the production of hormones, absorption of nutrients, and brain health. A line should be drawn between unhealthy trans fats and saturated fats, which are known to cause health problems, and healthy fats present in foods like avocados, nuts, seeds, and fatty fish. Emphasizing a balanced diet with healthy fats can support overall health and well-being.

Myth 4: Thinness Equals Fitness

Another very damaging myth is that thinness equates to fitness. The components of fitness include cardiovascular endurance, strength, flexibility, and overall physical activity levels. People of any size can be fit and active, and one should focus on functional movement and personal fitness goals, not body size.

Myth 5: Weight Stigma is Motivating

For too long, many have hoped-weight loss promotion; that is, discrimination by weight-can motivate overweight people to lose weight and develop better health. Evidence reveals it can have the opposite effects, leading to increased levels of stress and anxiety and disordered eating habits. Instead of inspiring behavior change, stigma creates barriers to seeking help and reduces the likelihood of healthy behavior being promoted and sought after.

A knowledge of the science underlying body diversity is a real key toward a more accepting and sensitive perspective about health. Understanding genetics, along with how the environment influences certain features of our bodies, allows an appreciation of the singular qualities our body type will inherit.

Understanding weight-related and health-related myths also serves to help individuals question societies' expectations while embracing an alternate view of well-being that is more wholistic in approach.

CHAPTER 3
NUTRITION: FUELING YOUR BODY

Nutrition is a central component of health and well-being, literally fueling our bodies and brains. This chapter will review the basics of balanced nutrition and introduce mindful eating practices that help people develop a healthier relationship with food. By learning how to feed our bodies well, we can move toward embracing health beyond size and support overall wellness.

PRINCIPLES OF BALANCED NUTRITION

Balanced nutrition is far from just counting calories or observing some restrictive diets; it means understanding how to feed one's body what it needs to perform optimally. Following are the key principles for balanced nutrition:

1. Variety is Key

Variety is one of the hallmarks of good nutrition. Different foods provide different nutrients, and eating a wide variety of foods ensures that you get a complete range of vitamins, minerals, and other nutrients. Try to include a rainbow of colorful fruits and vegetables, whole grains, lean proteins, and healthy fats in your diet. This will not only improve nutritional intake but also make meals more interesting and satisfying.

2. Focus on Whole Foods

Whole foods are those that have been minimally processed and/or are closer to their natural state, and generally contain more nutrients than processed foods. Whole foods will help balance your intake of the vital nutrients while reducing added sugars, unhealthy fats, and artificial ingredients. Examples of whole foods include:

Fresh, frozen, or dried Fruits and Vegetables, packed with vitamins, minerals, and antioxidants.

- ***Whole Grains:*** Foods like brown rice, quinoa, oats, and whole wheat bread that provide fiber and essential nutrients.

- ***Lean Proteins:*** Sources such as poultry, fish, beans, lentils, tofu, and nuts that support muscle health and overall body function.

- ***Healthy Fats***: Avocados, olive oil, nuts, and seeds that provide essential fatty acids and support heart health.

3. Balance Macronutrients

A healthy diet has an appropriate balance of the macronutrient components: carbohydrates, proteins, and fats. Each of the macronutrient components has a very specific function in the body:

- ***Carbohydrates:*** Provide energy for the body. Include more complex carbohydrates like whole grains, fruits, and vegetables in your diet.

- ***Proteins:*** Are vitally needed by the body to build and repair tissues, make enzymes and hormones, and ensure healthy immune function. Inclusion of a variety in the diet ensures intake of all essential amino acids.

- ***Fats:*** Are an important part of hormone production, nutrient absorption, and brain health. Emphasize healthier fats while limiting saturated and trans fats.

4. Hydration Matters

The most forgotten part of nutrition is hydration. Water contributes greatly in almost every function of the body, from digestion to the circulation and regulation of temperature within the body. Drink enough water during the day, and try to include hydrating foods such as fruits and vegetables in your diet.

5. Listen to Your Body

Understanding the hunger and fullness signals of the body is one aspect of good nutrition. Learning to listen to the body aids in making informed choices with regards to when and what to eat. This intuitive approach fosters a much healthier relationship with food, hence allowing you to pay closer attention to nutritional needs.

MINDFUL EATING PRACTICES

It helps you pay attention to the sensation, taste, and feel of eating food, cultivate your love for food, and keep good eating habits. This process can be incorporated into daily life in order to improve general food relationships and help people eat healthier.

1. Slow Down and Savor

With our fast-paced life, it is often very easy to rush through meals without really enjoying them. Take the time to slow down and savor each bite. Chew your food thoroughly, appreciate the flavors and textures, and allow yourself to fully experience the meal. This practice enhances enjoyment, aids digestion, and helps you recognize when you are full.

2. Eliminate Distractions

Eating in front of the TV, a smartphone, or the computer at work can lead to mindless eating and overeating. Create an eating environment that is free from distractions, where you can spend time focusing on your meal. This allows for mindfulness of your meal and attention to your body's signals of hunger and fullness.

3. Engage Your Senses

Eating is more mindful, which means paying attention to and engaging all the senses to eat. Note the colors and smells of food, also the textures. Be attuned to the sound and sensations in your mouth while eating. Engaging one's senses should increase appreciation and enjoyment when eating.

4. Express Gratitude

Before meals, take a moment to express gratitude for the food on your plate. Acknowledging the effort that went into growing, preparing, and serving your meal can foster a deeper connection to your food and promote a positive mindset around eating.

5. Reflect on Your Feelings

Take time to listen to your feelings and thoughts about food. Are you hungry, bored, stressed, or is this a habit? Knowing how emotional triggers set off your eating may lead you to more mindful decisions and healthier coping mechanisms.

6. Allow Yourself to Enjoy Your Cravings

Mindful eating allows you to honor your cravings, not suppress them. You enjoy foods that you love in moderation, without labeling them as "bad" or "off-limits." This might help reduce feelings of deprivation and allow a healthier relationship with food.

Nutrition is a vital component of health, way beyond just counting calories or following a restrictive diet. The balance in nutrition, coupled with the use of principles for mindful eating, brings nourishment to our bodies toward a general wellness perspective. Holistic nutrition enables the body to be powered while simultaneously adopting a very positive attitude toward food.

CHAPTER 4
MOVEMENT FOR JOY, NOT PUNISHMENT

Movement is important in a culture that tends to equate exercise with punishment or an avenue to a body type. This chapter will explore how to find enjoyable physical activities and highlight the numerous benefits of movement for mental and physical health. By embracing movement as a source of joy rather than a chore, we can develop a healthier relationship with our bodies and improve our overall well-being.

FINDING ENJOYABLE PHYSICAL ACTIVITIES

The first step in redefining movement is through finding activities that you enjoy. When exercise is a source of pleasure, it is instinctive and will form part of your life, rather than some dreary obligation. Following are ways in which to find the right activities for yourself:

1. Explore Your Options

There are so many different types of physical activity, and what works for one person may not work for another. Take some time to explore a few options, such as:

- *Dance:* Either in a class format or dancing around in your living room, dance can be a very fun and expressive way to move one's body.
- *Walking or Hiking:* A very rejuvenating way to incorporate movement into your routine is by enjoying nature through walking or hiking. Swimming can be both enjoyable and invigorating because of the buoyancy of water. Yoga or Pilates: The practice of yoga or Pilates focuses on flexibility, strength, and mindfulness, thus setting them as excellent choices when thinking about a holistic approach toward movement.

- *Team Sports:* Joining a recreational league or playing casual games with friends can add a social element to your physical activity.

- *Martial Arts:* Engaging in martial arts can provide a sense of empowerment and discipline while promoting physical fitness.

2. Listen to Your Body

Pay attention to how all the different activities make you feel. Are you charged and happy after certain workouts are done with, or exhausted and resentful? It will send those signals-if you listen-so you can figure it out yourself which activities you'll enjoy and which ones will benefit your body. Remember, movement should be a good feeling-not painful and punishing.

3. Create Realistic Goals

Instead of having goals related to weight loss or aesthetic goals, set goals regarding enjoyment and personal growth. Examples include trying a new activity every month or devoting a certain amount of time per week to movement. These can help shift the focus from external validation to internal satisfaction.

4. Make It Social

Social aspects can make physical activities more enjoyable and motivating. Invite friends or family to join you in activities, or consider joining a group or class. The camaraderie and support of others can make movement feel more enjoyable and less isolating.

5. Be Playful

Re-awaken your playful self by adding fun and spontaneity into your movement routine. Do things you used to do as a child, such as playing tag, jumping on a trampoline, or riding a bike. Let yourself be playful, and you will find joy in moving again.

THE BENEFITS OF MOVEMENT FOR MENTAL AND PHYSICAL HEALTH

Exercising regularly leads to a number of benefits relating to mental and physical well-being. Knowing these advantages will further motivate you to adopt the habit of enjoying movement in life.

1. Mood and Mental Health

Physical activity has been shown to release endorphins, the body's natural mood elevators. The regular movement will help decrease anxiety and depression, elevate one's mood, and allow individuals to feel better overall. Activities can be self-rewarding in themselves: the better the mental health from moving, the more one wants to continue moving.

2. Better Intellectual Performance

It has also promoted improved cognitive function, better memorization, focused concentration, and creativity. Exercise increases the blood flow to the brain, which in turn enhances neuron growth and strengthens overall health of the brain. Thus, this could enhance productivity through fastened problem-solving skills.

3. Stress Reduction

Movement is one of the strongest mediators for stress release. Through exercise, cortisol, commonly associated with stress, decreases and one feels relaxed and composed. Be it a brisk walk, yoga, or a dance class, finding time for movement can be a great way to get rid of stress.

4. More Energy

Unlike the belief that exercise depletes energy, regular physical activity can enhance energy levels. Moving around increases circulation and oxygen flow to the muscles, leading to improved stamina and vitality. Over time, individuals who incorporate moving into their daily activities tend to feel more energized and less fatigued.

5. Improved Sleep Quality

Regular physical activity is related to better quality sleep. The activity can regulate sleeping patterns, which helps in falling asleep and staying asleep. Besides, the relaxation obtained from physical activity can add to a good night's sleep.

6. Improved Physical Health

Movement is very important to anyone looking to keep physically fit. Doing some form of exercise helps maintain weight, improves cardiovascular conditions, strengthens muscles and bones, increases flexibility, and promotes better body balance. All these lead to living longer and having a quality life.

7. More Awareness of the Body and Sureness

Pleasurable physical activities have the potential to foster a greater sense of body awareness and confidence. It is through the learning to appreciate one's body for its functional abilities, rather than its appearance that an individual typically develops a positive body image that leads to increased self-esteem and a more favorable attitude toward oneself.

Movement should be a source of pleasure, not punishment. This could be fostered further by exploring enjoyable physical activities and the many ways in which movement can benefit our mental and physical health. Let's reconsider our relationship with our bodies: Movement can be a joyful means of self-care and a form of expression.

CHAPTER 5
MENTAL HEALTH MATTERS

Mental health is an integral part of overall well-being, and it is deeply intertwined with our perceptions of ourselves and our bodies. This chapter will review the ways in which body image may affect mental well-being and effective strategies for building self-esteem and fostering body positivity. By addressing these crucial aspects of mental health, we can empower ourselves and others to embrace health beyond size.

THE IMPACT OF BODY IMAGE ON MENTAL HEALTH

Body image is the cognitive representation of the body, comprised of thoughts, emotions, and perceptions about the body that occur within the mind. It is shaped by social expectations and norms, media, and often personal experiences. Our body perception may therefore affect our mental health in a variety of ways that include:

1. Self-esteem and confidence

Low self-esteem often accompanies a negative body image and diminished confidence. Individuals that are not happy with their bodies can barely feel worthy or capable, leading to feelings of inadequacy. A lack of confidence will take its toll on personal and professional growth, relationships, and opportunities.

2. Anxiety and Depression

Negative body image can potentially lead to serious mental health concerns, such as anxiety and depression. The constant criticism of personal appearance may heighten levels of stress and emotional turmoil, creating the potential to initiate a vicious circle that leads to further negative self-talk and feelings, exacerbating the mental health challenges of the individual.

3. Disordered Eating Behaviors

The mental distress from poor body image is considered a factor in disordered eating behaviors like restriction, binge eating, and/or purging. These factors typically have been associated with desires on the part of individuals to try to meet the demands of sociocultural beauty standards and may also pose grave consequences on an individual's physical and psychological health. The connection between body image and eating disorders is interwoven, yet unmistakably negative perceptions about body happen to create hazardous behaviors.

4. Social Isolation

People with negative body image may avoid social contacts because of feeling ashamed or too embarrassed about how they look. Consequently, such isolation can lead to loneliness and worsen psychological health conditions. The feeling of fear of judgment or rejection stops people from participation in activities that were enjoyable for them earlier, hence depreciating the quality of their life further.

5. Effects on Relationships

It may also affect interpersonal relationships because persons who have body image problems tend to project their feelings onto others, which leads to misunderstandings and conflicts. Negative body image may inhibit intimacy because a person feels unworthy of love or acceptance.

STRATEGIES FOR BUILDING SELF-

ESTEEM AND BODY POSITIVITY

Building a positive body image and self-esteem are some of the key components of good mental health. Following are a few strategies that will help an individual build a healthier relationship with his or her body:

1. Challenge Negative Thoughts

One of the first steps toward body positivity is challenging negative thoughts and beliefs about your body. When you find yourself criticizing your body, stop and reframe those thoughts. Instead of perceived flaws, consider what your body does for you and the unique qualities that make you who you are. The practice of self-compassion and kindness can help to change your perspective.

2. Surround Yourself with Positivity

The people and media we surround ourselves with can hugely impact our body image. Surround yourself with supportive friends and family members who uplift and encourage you. Also, curate your social media feeds to include body-positive accounts that celebrate diversity and promote self-acceptance. Positive messages counteract negative influences and help to reinforce a healthier perspective.

3. Practice Gratitude for Your Body

Appreciate your body: Gratitude can help you foster a good body image. Take the time daily to think of things you are thankful about your body, whether strong, resilient, or a vessel that can feel and take in pleasures. Keep a body gratitude journal to start redirecting the focus from appearance to function and wellness.

4. Do Things with Your Body

Positive body activities can help build self-esteem and create a sense of community. Find groups or classes that focus on the joys of movement, such as dancing, yoga, and aerobics. Participation in these activities with people who share similar values provides a supportive environment that will promote self-acceptance.

5. Seek Professional Support

If negative body image and low self-esteem significantly impact your mental health, consider seeking support from a mental health professional. Therapy can provide a safe space to explore your feelings and develop coping strategies. Cognitive-behavioral therapy (CBT) is particularly effective in addressing negative thought patterns and fostering a more positive self-image.

6. Focus on Health, Not Appearance

Shift your focus from appearance-based goals to health-oriented ones. Instead of focusing on achieving a particular weight or body shape, put your attention into specific actions that promote health: taking good care of your body through healthy foods, enjoyable exercises, and self-care. That way, you'll create a better relationship with yourself and not pay as much attention to your appearance.

7. Appreciate Diversity

Appreciate the diversity in body shapes and sizes. Not everyone fits into the small circle of beauty, and not everyone should. Love your uniqueness and respect the uniqueness of others, despite the so-called societal norms. This can help one foster a more inclusive and compassionate view of body image.

Mental health matters much in our journey to understand and embrace health beyond size. By understanding the effects that body image has on the mind, and by developing ways to establish self-confidence and body positivity, we can, in turn, create environments that are both supportive and empowering for ourselves and others. Treating our bodies with kindness and acceptance allows for the fostering of a more positive relationship with oneself, enabling better mental health and general well-being. Let us forge ahead in a way that keeps mental health to the fore and embraces diversity in all its glory.

CHAPTER 6
THE ROLE OF COMMUNITY AND SUPPORT

Community and support are invaluable on the journey toward understanding and embracing health beyond size. A strong network can provide encouragement, enhance resilience, and offer a sense of belonging. This chapter will consider how to develop a supportive network and focus on shared experiences and encouragement as a tool in overall well-being.

BUILDING A SUPPORTIVE NETWORK

Creating a supportive network involves surrounding yourself with individuals who uplift, inspire, and motivate you. This network can include friends, family, peers, and even online communities. Here are some strategies for building a robust support system:

1. Identify Your Needs

Before seeking support, take some time to consider what you need from your network: Are you looking for someone to offer emotional support, hold you accountable, or participate in activities with? When you know what you want, you'll know better who to have in your support circle.

2. Find People Like You

Look for people with similar values, goals, and experiences. These could be health-conscious friends, understanding relatives, or community groups that promote body positivity and wellness. Getting along with like-minded people builds companionship and a feeling of mutual understanding.

3. Find Support Groups

You can also consider joining physical or online support groups focused on body positivity, mental health, and wellness. Support groups are an opportunity for people to share experiences and advice among those who understand the situation much better. Most organizations offer forums and other resources that help you find community support.

4. Open Up Communication

Building a supportive network requires openness in communication. Share with the network your goals, challenges, and successes. Let them do the same, which will build trust in relationships and be a sound foundation for support.

5. Be a Source of Support

Support goes both ways. While seeking support from others, be willing to offer your encouragement and understanding as well. Being a source of support for others not only strengthens your relationships but also reinforces your own commitment to health and well-being.

6. Use Social Media Wisely

Social media is a powerful tool to build community. Follow body-positive accounts, join online forums, and engage in discussions that resonate with your journey. Be cautious, though, of what you are consuming. Curate your feed to reflect positive, uplifting messages that mirror your values.

7. Workshops and Events

Attendance or participation in workshops, seminars, and community events concentrated on health and wellness introduces the opportunity to meet and communicate with others of similar interests. Such gatherings let participants learn, share their experiences, and get to know other people who are on the same paths as themselves.

THE IMPORTANCE OF SHARED EXPERIENCES AND ENCOURAGEMENT

Shared experiences and encouragement are at the heart of a sense of community and belonging. Here are some reasons why these elements play an important role in maintaining good well-being:

1. Validation and Understanding

Sharing experiences will help people to at least feel a sense of validation and understanding. Knowing that others have faced similar challenges may help alleviate feelings of isolation and self-doubt. Such shared understanding encourages empathy and compassion, enabling the person to feel seen and heard.

2. Motivation and Accountability

A supportive network's encouragement is a potent driver. Individuals sharing their goals and progress are more likely to remain responsible for their path. Celebration of success, no matter how minor, reinforces behaviors in the right direction and provides the feeling of achievement.

3. Learning from Others

Shared experiences present golden opportunities from which so much can be learned. Listening to people's struggles, how they outsmart barriers, and how they feel when they win can hint at perspectives that might prove pertinent to one's own struggles. The exchange of information will help facilitate making decisions about personal health and well-being.

4. Building Resilience

A supportive community helps them develop resilience in bad times. When challenges occur, a network of people offering encouragement and support helps in the coping process regarding setbacks. This will help in maintaining motivation on the path of health and well-being.

5. Creating a Sense of Belonging

A sense of belonging is a connection to others from similar backgrounds and values, enabling one to feel a particular connectedness and acceptance. The feeling of belonging can be a promoter of good mental well-being, reducing feelings associated with loneliness and isolation. Therefore, it is when people receive support and acceptance that they are likely to engage themselves in healthy behaviors for wellbeing.

6. Body Positivity

Shared experiences and motivation in a supportive environment evoke feelings of body positivity and self-acceptance. The celebration of bodies of all shapes and sizes challenges societal norms to allow inclusivity to prevail among diverse cultures. This, altogether, will help break down a few stereotypical thoughts that are harmful and progress forward with a positive viewpoint towards health and beauty.

7. Enhanced Overall Well-being

Ultimately, this is a strong support network based on shared experiences and encouragement that increases well-being. Persons who feel supported are more liable to increase healthy behaviors, practice healthy self-care, and display an optimistic outlook on their lives. This holistic approach to health includes overall well-being in terms of their physical, mental, and emotional good health.

Communities and support are essential building blocks for understanding and ultimately accepting health beyond size. Let's create together with me a support network based on the recognition of communal experiences and encouragement. Let this be a place where personal growth, resilience, and well-being will thrive.

CHAPTER 7
NAVIGATING DIET CULTURE

Diet culture can be overwhelming in today's world, filled as it is with dieting and weight loss messages and ideal body types. The chapter will unpack the complications around diet culture, look into the effects it may bring about in individuals and society, and consider some strategies to be employed for informed choices amidst societal pressure. By understanding the pervasive nature of diet culture, we can develop a healthier, more balanced way of well-being with respect to our relationship with food and our bodies.

UNDERSTANDING DIET CULTURE AND ITS EFFECTS

Diet culture is a societal framework that equates thinness with health, beauty, and worth. It encompasses a wide range of beliefs, practices, and norms that focus on weight loss and body size over overall health and well-being. Understanding diet culture is key to recognizing how it influences our lives and those around us.

1. The Origins of Diet Culture

Diet culture has its deep roots in history, and over centuries, it shaped societal perception about body image and health. The fashion industry, media portrayal of beauty, and commercialization of weight loss are all contributing factors that have made diet culture pervasive. Today, it takes on many forms: social media trends, celebrity endorsements, and normalizing restrictive eating practices.

2. The Psychological Impact

The effects of diet culture on mental health can be profound. Constant exposure to idealized body images and messages about weight can lead to:

- ***Body Dissatisfaction:*** Many individuals develop a negative body image, feeling inadequate or unworthy due to their size or shape. This dissatisfaction can lead to a cycle of self-criticism and unhealthy behaviors.

- ***Disordered Eating:*** The culture of dieting encourages restraint while eating; this may lead to the precipitation of disordered eating behaviors like binge eating, emotional eating, or chronic dieting. Each of these can have serious consequences on both physical and psychological levels.

- ***Anxiety and Depression:*** These pressures of maintaining the beauty standards of society further deteriorate anxiety and depression due to continuous comparisons. They get overwhelmed and might start thinking of themselves as worthless.

3. Physical Consequences

The diet culture has several devastating consequences not only to the mental health but also on the body as well. A few major ones are :

- ***Nutritional deficiencies:*** Severely restrictive diets exclude a whole category of food from the intake, which makes nutrition imbalanced. This may include complications such as fatigue and weakened immunity due to this very reason. Yo-yo dieting: The normal cycle of weight loss followed by weight gain, commonly referred to as yo-yo dieting, could bring a metabolsim process into chaos even to an effect on long-term weight gain. This could further make one feel like a failure or frustrated.

- *Health Misconceptions:* Diet culture teaches people that weight alone is equated with health. This notion may push other important indicators of healthy mental well-being, fitness, and overall lifestyle out of one's focus.

4. The Social Effects

Diet culture touches on more than just a place of personal influence; it has created cultural touchstones. Thinness is virtuous, and larger bodies are shamed. Such thinking leads to systemic discrimination and prejudice in a way that impacts an individual trying to access healthcare, seek employment, or partake in social relations, and further adds to marginalization.

HOW TO MAKE INFORMED CHOICES AMIDST SOCIETAL PRESSURES

It is a process in which choice must be constantly made for the good of one's health and well-being against the pressures of diet culture. Following are a number of strategies to reclaim your relationship with food and your body:

1. Practice Critical Thinking

Critical thinking will help you to sort through the diet culture. You need to question messages coming from the media, advertising, and social interactions. Consider their motivations and if they truly align with your values and goals. By being critical, you will be better positioned to determine what is helpful for health.

2. Focus on Health, Not Weight

Shift your focus to overall health and well-being, rather than weight loss. Health is multi-dimensional: physical, mental, emotional. Focus on behaviors promoting wellness, such as nutrition, movement, and self-care, rather than striving for that magic number on the scale.

3. Practice Intuitive Eating

Intuitive eating is an approach to honoring one's body by listening to and honoring the body's hunger and fullness cues. This, in turn, fosters a healthier relationship with food and is characterized by being absolutely sure about a wide range of food enjoyment without any guilt or restriction. Core concepts of intuitive eating include:

- ***Rejecting the Diet Mentality:*** Realize that one does not need diets or a set of rules to follow regarding food.

Also helpful is to listen to your body's cues-when it says feed it with food; this means honor your hunger. Make Peace with Food: Allow yourself to eat all foods without the feeling of guilt or shame.

4. Surround Yourself with Positive Influences

Look for communities and people that foster body positivity and health at every size. Consume content that celebrates diversity in body shapes and sizes, and fight negative weight and health narratives. Surrounding yourself with positive influences can help reinforce a healthier mindset and provide support in your journey.

5. Educate Yourself

Take some time to learn about nutrition, health, and diet culture. Understanding the science of nutrition empowers you with better choices that will align more precisely with your values. Make sure the information taken is from a reputable source: a registered dietitian, any other health professional, or an evidence-based literature review.

6. Set Boundaries

Set boundaries around conversations or content about dieting or body image. Say no to conversations that steer into negative body talk or diet culture. Protecting your space will help you stay positive and focused on health beyond size.

7. Seek Professional Guidance

If you are feeling lost regarding diet culture or disordered eating behaviors, a professional will be able to work through those issues with you. For more detailed guidance and support, as individually appropriate, consult with a registered dietitian, therapist, or counselor.

Diet culture is complex and can sometimes be very overwhelming; however, doing so will be one of the first steps toward developing a much healthier relationship with food and our bodies. By understanding the pervasive nature of diet culture and its results, we are better able to make active choices serving our well-being rather than forcing societal pressures. Embracing a holistic approach in health and critical thinking for life, along with keeping company with supportive communities, allows us to reclaim our stories and celebrate our bodies in all of their difference.

CHAPTER 8
PERSONAL STORIES OF TRANSFORMATION

These personal stories of transformation, as in the journey to understand and embrace health beyond size, have given powerful reminders of resilience and courage through many different pathways individuals take towards attaining well-being. The chapter emphasizes inspiring stories from people who embraced their bodies and took a different view of mainstream standards while caring for themselves based on personal experiences that connect with their lives. Through these stories, we will grasp the lessons learned and the insights drawn, showing deep impacts brought forth by self-acceptance and holistic health.

INSPIRING STORIES FROM INDIVIDUALS EMBRACING HEALTH BEYOND SIZE

1. Sarah's Journey to Self-Acceptance

Sarah, a 32-year-old graphic designer, had always struggled with her body image. She grew up in a culture that put a great deal of emphasis on thinness and felt immense pressure to meet these unrealistic standards. After years of yo-yo dieting and beating herself up, Sarah finally reached her breaking point.

She found body positivity through social media as she began to search for ways of self-acceptance. Sarah started changing her view when she started following various accounts that celebrated the diverse shapes and sizes of the human body. She began practicing intuitive eating, nourishing her body rather than restricting it. Over time, Sarah learned to appreciate her body for strength and capabilities rather than appearance.

Today, Sarah is a body positivity activist who shares her journey on her blog to inspire others to love their bodies and take care of their mental health. Her story really shows the power of finding community and how beauty standards need to be redefined.

2. Mark's Movement Transformation

Mark was 45 and had been fighting his whole life with being overweight. A father of two decided he wanted to stop getting beat up by diet culture and instead just find joy in movement.

Mark started exploring all kinds of physical activities, from hiking to dancing, and then found his interest in rock climbing. This love for movement definitely changed his perception about the body. Rather than treating exercise as a punishment, he enjoyed his strength and resilience as a means to celebrate it.

In this process, Mark learned that health is not defined by a number on the scale but by the joy and fulfillment that physical activity brings. He now encourages others to find activities they love, emphasizing that movement should be enjoyable and empowering.

3. Lisa's Holistic Approach to Wellness

Lisa, 28, is a nutritionist who had her own share of body image and disordered eating. After years of going on restrictive diets, she realized that her approach towards health was not only unsustainably but also damaging for her well-being.

Lisa's determination for change finally sought a holistic approach toward her well-being, which incorporated all other aspects: nutrition, mental, and emotional health. She started to become more mindful and compassionate, letting her body's voice be heard without judgments.

Through this journey, Lisa learned the importance of balance and moderation within her diet. She now places a great emphasis on mental health in her practice, enabling clients to foster a positive relationship with food and their bodies. Lisa's story really underlines the transformative power of embracing such a holistic view of health.

4. James' Plea for Inclusion

James is an activist, 35-year-old, who has always been interested in social justice. Having faced discrimination because of his size, he became determined to fight for inclusivity and body acceptance.

James founded a community-based organization to promote body confidence and to question the mainstream concepts of health and beauty. He has provided a platform for people of all sizes to share their stories and experiences through workshops, events, and social media campaigns.

Through activism, his work has allowed others to be empowered by him while he, too, changed his relationship with his body. James will learn that embracing health beyond size involves demanding systemic changes and building a culture of acceptance. That is the reason community and activism feature among the deepest elements of the self-acceptance process.

LESSONS LEARNED AND INSIGHTS GAINED

Personal stories in this chapter have lessons and insights to which anyone on a journey toward embracing health beyond size can relate. Key takeaways follow:

1. The Power of Self-Acceptance

The deep underlying lesson from these stories is that of self-acceptance. Learning to love our bodies as they are, not striving for an ideal that is unattainable, is a crucial step toward mental and emotional well-being. Self-acceptance engenders resilience and enables individuals to take care of their health in a manner that is valued.

2. Redefining Health

Health means far more than weight or an image; it is the way of being physically, mentally, and emotionally. From the stories, health is in the joy of movement, feeding the body on purpose, and nurturing a positive relationship with food. Redefining health allows individuals to stop working so diligently against cultural pressures and instead focus their efforts on holistic well-being.

3. The Importance of Community

Community is an essential aspect of the journey toward self-acceptance and well-being. Individuals in this chapter found strength and support from being connected with others in the same direction. In feeling accepted, being part of such a supportive network encourages one also to go on their own journey.

4. Challenging Societal Norms

This paper is not an attempt to lead to an uprising against this societal set standard of beauty and health in regards to an inclusive culture. The stories shared will show readers the need to include body positivity through advocacy and activism that tear down hurtful stereotypes. This sharing of stories empowers other people to go against the status quo and celebrate diversity.

5. Enjoyment in Movement

One of the most revolutionary features of embracing health beyond size is finding joy in movement. The stories will illustrate how physical activity should not be about means to an end but rather an enjoyable and empowering feature. By exploring activities that bring joy, a person can develop a positive relationship with their body and enhance overall well-being.

6. The Journey is Ongoing

It's a journey, not a destination. Everyone's journey is different, and some are not without setbacks. Their stories remind us that above all, self-compassion and patience will be important to carry along on our journeys. Health beyond size is a continuous process of growth, learning, and self-discovery.

Personal stories of transformation give insight into the resilience and strength that may have been part of each individual's journey toward embracing health beyond size. By sharing these stories, we can encourage others to push against societal norms, move forward in self-acceptance, and nurture a holistic perspective on well-being.

CHAPTER 9
ADVOCATING FOR INCLUSIVITY IN WELLNESS

The more we learn about health and wellness, the more we realize just how important inclusivity can be in each wellness journey. By supporting inclusivity in wellness, we do not just make the experience richer for people of all sizes; we nurture a culture of diversity in which holistic health thrives. This chapter will talk about the role of representation in health and wellness and offer some actionable steps toward inclusion in fitness and healthcare.

THE IMPORTANCE OF REPRESENTATION IN HEALTH AND WELLNESS

Representation in health and wellness is important for several reasons. It builds perceptions, informs behaviors, and dictates health outcomes for diverse populations. Some key aspects that underlie the importance of representation are discussed below.

1. Challenging Stereotypes

Representation in health and wellness helps challenge and dismantle some of these injurious stereotypes that correlate body size with health.

Representation in health-related media communicates a powerful message-that health is not limited to any single kind of body. It serves as a way to counter some stigma associated with larger persons, opening a view on health that encompasses a greater perspective than often currently considered.

2. Relatability

The moment people see themselves represented in health and wellness spaces, it automatically allows them to feel a connection toward relatability. Representation brings about connections and invites individuals into participation in practices that have something to say to them. Relatability will motivate more people to care about their health and wellness since their journeys, though unique, are of value.

3. Increasing Accessibility

Inclusive health and wellness also call for increased access to resources and facilities. When diverse bodies exist, it speaks to the kind of facilities that are needed for individuals irrespective of their size and abilities; hence, programs, structures, and services are eventually developed to be more accessible for all.

4. Normalizing Diverse Stories

Representation gives way to the sharing of a wide array of stories and experiences concerning health and wellness. These can be an integral source of insight into the problems and successes that different groups encounter. In giving voice to these stories, we may promote a deeper understanding of health than the traditional metrics can capture and truly appreciate the nuance of individual experiences.

5. Inspiring Change

Representation in health and wellness could be the impetus to urge people into making change within their communities. Maybe representation would provide an avenue for people to start pushing against the grain, demanding inclusivity and asking for policies and practices that truly consider the well-being of all individuals, regardless of their size or background.

HOW TO PROMOTE INCLUSIVITY IN FITNESS AND HEALTHCARE

It requires some serious commitment: being inclusive within the context of fitness and health necessitates intentionally creating environments welcoming to individuals of all shapes and sizes. The following suggestions may help with inclusivity in such places:

1. Professional Training

Health professionals, fitness professionals, and wellness professionals should be trained regarding body diversity, size acceptance, and the principles of HAES. Education may allow professionals to understand the need for inclusion and provide them with tools to approach individuals of all sizes with compassion and respect.

2. Create Inclusive Spaces

Gyms and healthcare spaces should ensure that environments are welcoming. This includes:

- *Diverse Representation:* Showcase images and materials that represent all shapes, sizes, and backgrounds. Sometimes, the only way people feel included is through the visual representations.

- *Accessible Equipment:* Make sure exercise equipment is accessible to individuals of all sizes and abilities. This includes providing options regarding equipment and ensuring spaces physically can accommodate all.

- *Inclusive Language:* Using language in marketing materials, communications, and interpersonal contact that includes all shapes and sizes and avoids language that stigmatizes or marginalizes individuals based on size.

3. Offer Diverse Programming

Exercise and wellness programs should be representative of the diversity within the community they serve. This could include:

- *Types of Classes:* Offer classes that cater to all interest levels, abilities, and body types. Consider offering low-impact classes, adaptive classes, and active programs for raising awareness about body acceptance.

- *Community Engagement:* Empower the community and involve them in creating programming and services. Ask questions on an ongoing basis as a way to assure yourself that the program offerings match their needs and interests.

4. Advocate for Policy Change

Well-rounded activism for inclusivity in wellness also covers systemic changes. This can involve health policies that will ensure people of all sizes have access to healthcare and wellness resources. This might be done in conjunction with local and national groups to help effect policy changes.

- *Insurance Coverage:* Advocate for insurance to cover a variety of wellness services, including nutrition counseling, mental health support, and fitness programs, regardless of body size.

5. Create Community Support

Community building is one important way to create an inclusive wellness environment. This may include:

- *Support Groups:* Organize or lead support groups that promote body positivity and self-acceptance along with overall holistic health. This can give them an area wherein people feel at home amongst their peers, having personal time to share in a non-judgmental way.

- *Events of Collaboration:* Engage in various body types, shape-, and size-neutral opportunities within the community through workshops, health fairs, and fitness challenges-anything at all.

6. Share Your Story

Allow people to share their personal stories of health and wellness. Such stories put a face to the issue of body diversity and help others understand that not everyone's path is comparable. Sharing of stories can be done on social media, blogs, podcasts, and community events.

7. Challenge Discrimination

Speak out against discrimination and prejudice in fitness and healthcare. This may include:

- ***Reporting Mechanisms:*** Encourage reporting of instances of discrimination or bias in the wellness spaces one may frequent. This helps create some degree of accountability.

- ***Raise Awareness:*** Through social media and community, raise awareness about the effect of discrimination and the essence of inclusivity in wellness.

Inclusivity in wellness is a crucial step to a healthy and equal society. By recognizing the importance of representation in health and wellness, and by implementing strategies for creating inclusive fitness and healthcare settings, we can develop settings where diversity is celebrated and all-size individuals are empowered in developing healthy lifestyles.

CHAPTER 10
UNDERSTANDING EMOTIONAL EATING

Emotional eating is a complex phenomenon, affecting many individuals, big and small. It's using food to solve one's emotions, stress, or difficulties in life rather than for satisfying the root cause of hunger. The next chapter deals with the detailed relation between emotions and food intake and will bring forth the psychological factors responsible for emotional eating. We will also be sharing practical ways of developing mindful eating practices and increasing emotional awareness that will help in building a better relationship with food.

EXPLORING THE CONNECTION BETWEEN EMOTIONS AND EATING HABITS

1. The Nature of Emotional Eating

Emotional eating is when one uses food as a way of comforting, distracting, or resolving negative emotions. This can take many forms, such as:

- *Eating in Response to Stress:* Many people find themselves reaching for snacks or comfort foods during stressful situations, using food as a way to cope with anxiety or overwhelm.

- *Using Food as a Reward:* Some individuals associate food with positive emotions, using it as a reward for accomplishments or as a way to celebrate special occasions.

- *Eating to Avoid Emotions:* Food may serve as a means of diverting one's attention from unwanted feelings of sadness, loneliness, or anger. Here, one eats in order to divert or avoid one's emotional state rather than confronting it head-on.

2. The Psychological Factors Involved

Some of the psychological factors for emotional eating are:

Food can also become associated with comfort and reward from early in life; thus, conditioning habits that will prevail over into adult years as a consistent emotional eater. For many people, it's not uncommon that overeating is merely the chosen primary coping mechanism against stress, anxiety, and depression; every time uncomfortable emotions present themselves, the food option starts to work for one.

- *Body Image Issues:* Poor body image and feeling not good enough may increase tendencies for emotional eating. People who feel bad about themselves often turn to food as a means of dealing with self-perceived worthless feelings and dissatisfaction.

- *Social Influences:* Cultural and social factors can also contribute to emotional eating. For example, cultural associations of food with celebration or consolation may support the belief that eating is a suitable reaction to emotional distress.

3. The Cycle of Emotional Eating

Emotional eating can be a self-perpetuating cycle. It usually involves:

- *Triggering Events:* Stressful events, negative emotions, or certain triggers of any kind may lead a person to Food.

- *Eating for Relief:* Then, these triggers lead an individual to emotional eating. The person starts eating due to his discomfort.

- *Feelings of Guilt or Shame:* After that incident of emotional eating, the person experiences feelings of guilt or shame, which leads to negative self-talk and further emotional distress.

- *Reinforcing the cycle:* emotional pain and guilt contribute to starting the cycle anew-a return to food as one's comfort zone.

STRATEGIES FOR MINDFUL EATING AND EMOTIONAL AWARENESS

This does require effort in developing a better relationship with food and getting oneself out of the vicious cycle of emotional eating. Following are a few strategies to help people develop mindful eating and become more emotionally aware.

1. Practice Mindful Eating

The principle of mindful eating encourages being present during meals to fully experience both food and one's body. The main points for eating mindfully are:

- *Stop Rushing:* Relish every bite, noticing taste, texture, and aroma; slowing down can also promote discovery over the body's signs about hunger and fullness.

- *Get Rid of Distractions:* Eat in a very comforting environment with minimal distractions from the television, smartphones, work, or anything that ruins focusing time in a meal. This gives a greater awareness to and increase of pleasures within meals.

- *Listen to the Hunger Cues:* While planning to eat, take time and evaluate your physical hunger state. Ask yourself whether you really feel hungry or are eating to distract yourself from emotional needs or external food cues.

2. Emotional Awareness

To develop emotional awareness, it will provide insight into the inner motivators for emotional eating. Development of emotional awareness can be fostered through the following activities:

- *Food and Feelings Journal:* Record eating and emotions in a food and feelings journal. Include circumstances around meals, such as emotional states, triggers, and cravings. This can help identify patterns and raise self-awareness.

- *Identify Triggers:* Reflect on what situations or emotions trigger emotional eating. By being more aware of the triggers, individuals can find other ways of dealing with their feelings rather than turning to food.

- *Practice self-compassion*: treat yourself with kindness and empathy when eating emotionally. Realize it's normal behavior, and beating yourself up over it may fuel guilty and shameful feelings.

3. Develop Alternative Coping Strategies

Finding alternative ways to cope with emotions can help break the cycle of emotional eating. Consider the following strategies:

- *Get Moving:* Physical activity is another pretty helpful method of dissipating stress and soothing your mood. Find what works for you, whether that be walking, dancing, yoga, or even just moving.

- *Practice Relaxation Techniques:* Make deep breathing, meditation, or some sort of mindfulness part of your day. These can help cut down on stress and improve your emotional balance.

- *Connect with Others:* Reach out to friends, family, or support groups when feeling overwhelmed. Social connections can provide emotional support and help alleviate feelings of loneliness or isolation.

4. Create a Supportive Environment

A supportive environment may promote healthier eating and emotional well-being. Here are some ways:

Stock Healthy Options: Keep in the house a variety of healthy options. Healthy snacking and meals will decrease the overindulging that is common when using food for emotional eating.

- ***Establish Meal Routines:*** Keep consistency with mealtimes and snacks to create a routine sense about the experience. It may also differentiate between being hungry physically or craving due to emotional triggers.

- ***Seek Professional Help:*** If emotional eating becomes too much to handle, seek help from a registered dietitian, therapist, or counselor. Professional guidance can provide valuable insights and strategies tailored to the individual.

CHAPTER 11
THE IMPACT OF MEDIA AND SOCIETY

The media has the power to shape norms and values about body image, which has consequences for communities. Images of bodies that are used in television, films, advertisements, social networking sites, and other mass media bring great influence in personal outlooks on himself or others. This chapter explores a variety of ways that media images can influence body image, and proposes practical strategies to promote a more critical engagement with media.

HOW MEDIA REPRESENTATIONS AFFECT BODY IMAGE

1. The Power of Representation

Media representations greatly influence body image because often, they set standards on what is considered attractive, healthy, or desirable. Such representations may manifest in a variety of ways:

- *Idealized body types:* Often, the media have a very small version of what good looks mean; they often portray very thin and toned conventionally attractive bodies, which can make people feel inefficient or unsatisfied with their personal bodies, thus developing negative feelings about their body image.

Stereotyping and marginalization are two common ways that media portray larger bodies, often using them in negative or comedic contexts. This kind of marginalization will only serve to solidify these biases in society and make size-based stigmatization worse.

- *Lack of diversity:* when the media do not show a wide variety of body shapes, colors, and abilities, persons who lack the stereotype can feel somehow left out. Due to a lack of exposure of this in media, different groups, especially the minorities, experience low self-esteems and feelings of invisible existence.

2. Effects on Body Image - Psychological Effects

The representations in media about body image are not superficial; rather, they affect an individual's life psychologically:

- *Internalization of Standards:* There are also possibilities that when idealized images are viewed repeatedly, they will be internalized into individual cognitions, leading to body dissatisfaction and unhealthy behaviors. These may be in the forms of disordered eating or excessive exercise and other destructive habits to achieve an impossible ideal.

- *Comparison Culture:* Social media, in particular, propagates a comparison culture wherein individuals take to gauging their worth by the curated life and bodies of others. It is continuous comparisons that cause hurt feelings and low self-esteem.

- *Mental Health Implications:* Poor body image is associated with a range of psychiatric disturbances, including anxiety, depression, and eating disorders. The pressure to maintain the appearance of beauty may result in a vicious circle of self-criticism and emotional turmoil.

3. The Role of Social Media

Social media has revolutionized how people interact with body image and standards of beauty:

- *Influencer culture:* social media influencership has created new beauty ideals that at times are impossible to realize, with uncritical standards of body parameters being set. Thus, many influencers create their images in a polished and idealized version, distorting the reality for their followers.

- *Filters and Editing:* The promotion of filters and photo editing further fosters unattainable beauty standards. The consequence of this can be the pressures people put on themselves to meet the expectations of these doctored images, leaving them discontented with how they look in reality.

- *Community and Support*: On the other hand, social media can also be used to foster positive body image and self-acceptance. The success of various grassroots movements that celebrate shapes and sizes and defy classic beauty ideals has given participants an opportunity to acquire this sense of community and recognition.

STRATEGIES FOR CRITICAL MEDIA CONSUMPTION

To navigate the complex landscape of media representations and their impact on body image, it is essential to develop critical media consumption skills. Here are several strategies to empower individuals to engage with media more thoughtfully:

1. Cultivate Media Literacy

Media literacy involves the ability to critically analyze and evaluate media messages. Key components of media literacy include:

- *Questioning Representations:* Encourage individuals to question the representations they encounter in media. Ask critical questions such as: Who created this content? What message is being conveyed? Whose voices are included or excluded?

- *Recognizing Bias:* Be aware of the biases that may influence media portrayals. Understand that media often reflects societal norms and values, which can perpetuate stereotypes and narrow definitions of beauty.

2. Diversify Media Consumption

Expanding the range of media consumed can help counteract the effects of narrow beauty standards:

- *Seek Diverse Voices:* Actively seek out media that features diverse body types, ethnicities, and experiences. This can include films, television shows, books, and social media accounts that celebrate body positivity and inclusivity.

- *Support Body-Positive Content:* Engage with creators and influencers who promote body positivity and challenge traditional beauty norms. Supporting these voices can help amplify messages of acceptance and diversity.

3. Limit Exposure to Negative Media

Reducing exposure to media that promotes unrealistic beauty standards can help protect against negative body image:

- *Unfollow Toxic Accounts:* On social media, curate your feed by unfollowing accounts that promote harmful beauty ideals or engage in body shaming. Instead, follow accounts that inspire and uplift.

- *Take Breaks from Social Media:* Consider taking regular breaks from social media to reduce the pressure of constant comparison. Use this time to engage in activities that promote self-care and self-acceptance.

4. Practice Self-Compassion

Developing self-compassion is essential for countering the negative effects of media representations:

- *Challenge Negative Thoughts:* When negative thoughts about your body arise, practice challenging these thoughts with self-compassion. Remind yourself that your worth is not determined by your appearance.

- *Focus on Health and Well-Being:* Shift the focus from appearance to overall health and well-being. Engage in activities that promote physical, mental, and emotional health, regardless of body size or shape.

5. Engage in Conversations

Open discussions about media representations and body image can foster awareness and understanding:

- ***Talk About Media Influence:*** Engage in conversations with friends, family, or support groups about the impact of media on body image. Sharing experiences and perspectives can help individuals feel less isolated in their struggles.

- ***Advocate for Change:*** Support initiatives that promote diversity and inclusivity in media. Advocate for more accurate and varied representations of bodies in advertising, film, and television.

The impact of media and society on body image is profound and far-reaching. By understanding how media representations shape perceptions of beauty and self-worth, individuals can take proactive steps to cultivate a healthier relationship with their bodies. Through critical media consumption, self-compassion, and advocacy for diverse representations, we can challenge societal norms and create a more inclusive narrative around health and beauty.

CHAPTER 12
SETTING REALISTIC GOALS FOR HEALTH

Setting realistic health and wellness goals provides an important step toward the journey to embrace health beyond size. The goals give direction to, motivation, and a sense of purpose one may navigate through his or her path toward well-being. Approaching goal-setting requires attention toward sustainability and self-compassion in mindset. The discussion now centers around setting achievable health and wellness goals, including celebrating small accomplishments over time.

HOW TO SET ACHIEVABLE HEALTH AND WELLNESS GOALS

1. Know Your Starting Point

In setting goals, it is important to take stock of your health and wellness status. This includes:

- *Self-Reflection:* Take some time to reflect on your physical, emotional, and mental state. Take into consideration your eating behaviors, level of physical activity, handling of stress, and feelings of well-being.

- *Identify Strengths and Challenges:* Recognize your strengths and areas for improvement. This will enable you to set goals that are more realistic and relevant to you.

2. Use the SMART Framework

The SMART framework is an accepted way of setting effective goals. The acronym SMART stands for Specific, Measurable, Achievable, Relevant, and Time-bound. Here's how to use this framework:

- *Specific*: Clearly define what it is you want to achieve. Instead of

"I want to be healthier," your goal should be specific, such as "I want to eat more fruits and vegetables."

- *Measurable:* Establish a criterion to measure the progress. For example, "I will eat at least five servings of fruits and vegetables each day" makes for easy tracking.

- *Achievable:* Your goals should be feasible to attain considering your prevailing circumstances. Your lifestyle, resources, and commitments come into play here. For instance, since you presently exercise once a week, setting a goal of exercising five times a week may not be realistic. In its place, aim to exercise two to three times a week.

- *Relevant:* Your goals should be in tandem with your overall health and wellness goals. Ask yourself why this is an important goal to you and how this fits into your greater vision of health.

- *Time-bound:* Establish a timeline for when you want to achieve your goals. This puts a sense of urgency and accountability. For example, "I will add more fruits and vegetables into my diet for one month and reassess my changes."

3. Break Down Big Goals into Small Ones

Very big goals often make you feel overwhelmed; this way, it's hard to feel motivated with them. A breakdown can help in not only clearly envisioning tiny steps forward but also making practical, functional steps toward your goal. For example, going to a gym, joining a different class, and finding somebody to work out together with-that is how breaking down larger goals into smaller ones sounds.

- ***Setting Short-Term Goals:*** Besides setting long-term goals, set short-term goals achievable within weeks or months. These small-scale goals may be used as stepping stones toward the big ones.

4. Be Flexible and Adaptable

Life is unpredictable, and circumstances may change. It's essential to remain flexible and adaptable in your goal-setting approach:

- ***Re-evaluate Goals:*** The progress should be evaluated from time to time, and goals reconsidered. Change the goal if it no longer seems relevant or achievable.

- ***Learn from Setbacks:*** Understand that setbacks may also happen along the way. Rather than looking at them as failures, it is good to take them as opportunities to learn and grow. Modify the goal if necessary and move ahead in life.

5. Seek Support and Accountability

Having a support system can significantly enhance your goal-setting journey in the following ways:

- ***Share Your Goals:*** Communicate your goals with friends, family, or a support group. Sharing your aspirations can create a sense of accountability and encourage others to support you.

Take professional guidance in case of doubt or for wanting more: One may plan on visiting a registered dietician, personal trainer, or health coach-according to personal desire and comfort. They offer a person an individually personalized line for action and set achievable targets accordingly.

THE IMPORTANCE OF CELEBRATING SMALL VICTORIES

1. Building Motivation and Momentum

Celebrating small victories has to do with maintaining motivation and momentum on your journey of health:

- ***Acknowledge Progress:*** Recognizing and celebrating small achievements reinforces positive behavior and encourages continued effort. Whether it is drinking more water, completing a workout, or trying out a new healthy recipe, acknowledging these milestones can help boost your confidence.

- *Creating Positive Associations:* Celebrating small victories helps create positive associations with your health journey. By rewarding yourself after reaching your goal, you learn to find healthy behaviors rewarding and pleasurable.

2. Developing Self-Compassion

Celebrating small victories nurtures self-compassion and kindness to oneself:

Instead of dwelling on long-term goals or perceived failures, celebrating small victories lets you appreciate how far you have come. This shift in focus can help combat negative self-talk and foster a more positive self-image.

- **Practice Gratitude:** Take time to reflect on what you have achieved and be thankful for your efforts. This will go a long way in enhancing your overall well-being and fostering a more compassionate mindset.

3. Community Building

Celebrating small wins paves the way to a more united and connected atmosphere in relationships with others:

- *Sharing Success:* Success is always to be shared with your friends, family, or online communities. Sharing allows one to have the same support network that feels supported themselves to continue on toward reaching those goals.

- *Encourage Others:* Celebrating your own victories encourages others to acknowledge and celebrate their successes. These collective celebrations may spread on to bring a supportive culture of encouragement.

4. Reinforcing Long-Term Commitment

Celebrating small victories reinforces your commitment to long-term health and wellness:

- *Smarter Motivation:* Knowing this brings in more motivation and a leaning toward your goal. On those off days, sustained motivation pushes the individual to be strong to overcome challenges and setbacks.

- ***Cultivating a Positive Mindset:*** These tiny reasons to celebrate build positive mindsets. Thus, making every future goal easy to reach and with much enthusiasm, one increases the experience of a journey toward health.

Setting realistic health and wellness goals is one of the most significant elements of Health Beyond Size. Getting to know your starting point, applying the SMART model, breaking down big goals into small steps, remaining flexible, and seeking support are just some of the key elements to creating a map to success.

CHAPTER 13
BUILDING HEALTHY
RELATIONSHIPS WITH FOOD

Food is a big part of our lives; besides being a source of sustenance, it also connects us, celebrates us, and comforts us. But societal pressures and personal experiences can make our relationship with food complicated and lead to a negative pattern of eating, whereby one rewards or punishes oneself with food. In this chapter, we will look at the idea of understanding food as nourishment and not as a transactional element of reward versus punishment. In addition, we will give tips on how to develop a positive relationship with food that will enable one to embrace a healthier and more balanced relationship with food.

UNDERSTANDING FOOD AS NOURISHMENT, NOT A REWARD OR PUNISHMENT

1. The Role of Food in Our Lives

Food plays many roles other than providing nutrition. Food is a source of pleasure, a way of communicating, and a part of culture. But the way we think about food can greatly affect how we eat and our health:

- *Nourishment vs. Reward*: Viewing food strictly as a reward can create a vicious cycle of emotional eating. This is where a person eats in response to stress, sadness, or boredom. This way, one creates a very bad association with food and feelings, which leads to guilt and shame when consuming foods one considers forbidden.

- *Punishment and Restriction:* On the other hand, food can be used as a punishment-reward factor in life, which is where one may limit or label certain foods as "bad." This may nurture a negative relationship with eating, where feelings of deprivation might ultimately give in to binge eating or a cycle of restriction and overindulgence.

2. Reframing Our Relationship with Food

In our relationships with food, re-attuning of our mindsets plays an important role:

- *Food as Fuel:* Learn to regard food primarily as a substance that nourishes the body with the energy and nutrients that it needs. In putting emphasis on the role of food as fuel, the emotional focus would not be as overwhelming and concentrated on the benefits derived from good nutrition.

- *Mindful Eating:* eating in a state of awareness, paying attention to flavors and textures of food. Mindful eating allows one to enjoy their food more but also tune in to their hunger and fullness cues in their body so they can honor an intuitive way of eating.

- *Emotional awareness:* Know what emotions could make a person eat the food. Understanding how one overeats and identification of triggers to emotional eating will enable them to start using healthy ways of coping, such as engaging in physical activity, keeping a journal, or spending time with friends.

3. Variety and Balance

A healthy relationship to food is including variety and balance:

Variety in Foods: Allow yourself to enjoy all types of foods, including fruits, vegetables, whole grains, proteins, and healthy fats. Emphasizing variety can help one avoid feelings of deprivation and have a more positive attitude toward eating.

- *No "Good" or "Bad" Foods:* Challenge the preconceived idea of naming foods "good" or "bad." Realize all foods have a place in a healthy diet if eaten in moderation. This view promotes flexibility and diminishes guilt about indulgence in certain foods.

TIPS FOR FOSTERING A POSITIVE RELATIONSHIP WITH FOOD

It means intentionally building a relationship with food, which takes practice. Here are some concrete ways to develop a healthy connection with food:

1. Practice Intuitive Eating

One way is by intuitive eating-listening to and honoring the body by being in tune with the hunger-fullness cues:

- *Listening to Your Body:* Paying attention to your body's feeling of hunger and fullness. Normally eat when you are hungry and stop when satisfied, not because of external cues or rigid meal plans.

- *Desire for Food:* Trust your food craving; allow yourself to enjoy whatever is craved without guilt. Trusting your cravings puts one more in a position to maintain a balanced approach toward food and minimizes the possibilities of binge eating.

2. Eat in a Positive Environment

Your environment when you eat can make a big difference in your relationship with food:

- *Mindful Eating Space:* Prepare a comfortable, distraction-free space to have meals. This can heighten one's attention to the food and increase the experience of eating, thereby becoming more mindful and enjoying it more.

- *Share Meals:* Eating with the family or friends can produce a social feeling and will add delight. This helps in accepting food very positively and motivates eating behaviors.

3. Challenge the Negative Thoughts

Negative thinking about food and body may disrupt the positiveness of the relationship to eat:

- ***Cognitive Restructuring***: Challenging negative thoughts and beliefs about food and the body and reconstructing them as positive, real thoughts. For example, regarding dessert, "I should not eat dessert," may be framed more positively as "I can enjoy dessert in moderation as part of a balanced diet."

- ***Practice self-compassion:*** Be nice to yourself around food choices. Remember that everyone has those moments of indulgence, and it's important to approach those moments with self-compassion rather than guilt.

4. Focus on Cooking and Meal Preparation

Engaging in the cooking process can help improve your relationship with food:

- ***Experiment with Recipes:*** Try new recipes and cooking techniques to explore flavors and cuisines. Cooking is a way of being creative and thus enhancing appreciation for food.

- ***Involve Others:*** Invite your family or friends to prepare the meal together. Cooking can become a communal activity and more fun.

5. Educate Yourself About Nutrition

- ***Learn About Nutrients:*** Knowing what kind of nutrient value you are getting with your foods can help empower you toward making better choices. The more you know your nutrients and the role different foods play in your body, the better you will understand the important role food can play in nourishing your body.

- ***Avoid Diet Culture:*** Be leery of the diet culture, with a strong emphasis on food avoidance. Instead, promote education about balanced nutrition and enjoyment of many foods.

Healthy relationship with food is one very essential perspective of embracing health beyond size. Understanding food as nourishment rather than reward or punishment will help people achieve an attitudinally positive and much more balanced way of relating to eating. Praticing intuitive eating, making an enabling eating environment, challenging the negativisms, engaging in cooking, and learning about nutrition-all these can serve as the fundamental building blocks of this relationship.

CHAPTER 14
CREATING A SUSTAINABLE HEALTH JOURNEY

The health journey is very personal and can be transformational; it requires commitment not only to change but also thoughtfully in making sure the changes one makes can be maintained long into the future. In this chapter, we will explore how to develop a personalized plan for long-term success, and provide practical tips to help you stay motivated and accountable on your health journey.

DEVELOPING A PERSONALIZED PLAN FOR LONG-TERM SUCCESS

1. Assess Your Current Status

This is the initial, very important step in developing a personalized health plan based on your current assessment.

Assess your physical, emotional, and mental health. Make considerations for eating habits, exercise, management of stress, and presence of diseases. This evaluation will give a basis on which your personal plan will be developed.

- *Identify Your Goals:* Take a moment to consider what you want to reach by taking this journey into health. Your goals may revolve around better physical fitness, improved mental well-being, managing your stress levels, or healthier ways of eating. Be specific about what success will look and feel like to you.

2. Set Realistic and Achievable Goals

Setting realistic and achievable goals is the initial step toward long-term success:

Apply the SMART framework to your goals. Refer to Chapter 12 for details about SMART criteria: specific, measurable, achievable, relevant, time-bound. By this, goals will become more clearly in focus and also an easier process in which to measure success.

- ***Prioritize Your Goals:*** Some of the goals may be dearer to you than others. Prioritize them. You can only focus on a few key objectives at any one time without getting overwhelmed, and your chances of success will be higher.

3. Formulate a Balanced Action Plan

A balanced action plan outlines specific steps you will take in achieving your goals:

- ***Variety in Application:*** A plan should incorporate variety in its activities of physical, emotional, and mental development. This can be a combination of exercise, nutrition, stress management techniques, and self-care practices.

- ***Schedule Your Activities:*** Take your listed activities and place them in a weekly or monthly schedule. Scheduling specific times to exercise, cook meals, or bathe and relax can make the plan stick to your lifestyle.

- ***Be Flexible:*** Life is unpredictable, and it's essential to remain flexible in your approach. If something doesn't go as planned, be willing to adjust your schedule or modify your goals as needed.

4. Focus on Sustainable Changes

Sustainability is key to long-term success:

- ***Adopt Gradual Changes:*** Instead of making drastic changes to your lifestyle, focus on gradual adjustments that can be maintained over time. For example, if you want to increase your physical activity, start with short walks and gradually build up to longer workouts.

- ***Focus on Pleasure:*** Engage in activities and eat food that is pleasurable. You tend to continue a behavior that you enjoy doing. Try various forms of exercises, ways of cooking, and healthy recipes to find out what works for you.

5. Track Your Progress

Tracking your progress will help you stay on the right path:

- *Journal Record:* You could keep a health journal whereby you record your goals, activities, and feelings over the course of the journey. This may be quite helpful in that it allows for reflection and the identification of patterns that take place in behavior.

- *Celebrating Successes:* Remember to celebrate successes, no matter how minute they may be. It will reinforce your motivations and commitments toward the health journey.

TIPS FOR MAINTAINING MOTIVATION AND ACCOUNTABILITY

Staying motivated and accountable throughout your journey is what gets you over the long term. Here are several practical tips for maintaining commitment:

1. Find Your "Why"

Understand your underlying reasons for a powerful source of inspiration:

- *Get Clear About Your Values:* Think about what health means to you and why it is important. Whether improving quality of life, having more energy, or simply setting a good example for those you love, identifying your "why" can help in the refocusing process.

- *Visualize Your Success:* Take time to visualize what achieving your goals will look and feel like. Creating a mental image of your success can serve as a motivating reminder of what you're working toward.

2. Build a Support Network

Having a support system can significantly enhance your motivation and accountability:

- ***Share Your Goals:*** Share your health goals with your friends, family, or any support group. By sharing your aims, you may develop some sense of responsibility and let others support and encourage you toward your goals.

- ***Connect with Similar-Minded People:*** Find a community or group of people with the same health goals as you. Connecting with others who are like-minded in their journey may provide encouragement, inspiration, and a sense of belonging.

3. Create Ways to Keep Yourself Accountable

Accountability will keep you on the right track:

- ***Find an Accountability Partner:*** It would be great to collaborate with a friend, family member, or a coach who can help you be responsible with your goals. Regular checks-ins will motivate and support you.

- ***Use Technology:*** Use apps or online platforms to track your progress and set reminders for your activities. Many apps offer features for logging meals, workouts, and other health-related behaviors, making it easier to stay accountable.

4. Embrace a Growth Mindset

A growth mindset fosters resilience and adaptability:

- ***View Setbacks as Opportunities***: Consider setbacks as opportunities for more learning and growth. Challenges can indeed be used as a means to nurture resilience and motivation within an individual.

- ***Practice Self-Compassion:*** Be compassionate towards yourself when you are challenged. Remember that everyone has issues with their health, and it may be useful to approach your own self with acceptance and compassion.

5. Regular Reevaluation of Goals

As you move along in your journey, it's a good idea to reevaluate your goals periodically. Here's how:

- ***Evaluate Your Progress:*** Sometimes revisit your goals to assess how you're doing. Celebrate your successes, and identify what, if anything, you'd like to do differently.

- ***Adjust Goals as Necessary:*** Be prepared to change your goals as your situation changes. That is simply part of the process in creating a health journey that will be sustainable for you.

A sustainable health journey will be about developing a personalized plan that reflects one's unique goals and values. It all comes down to assessing where one is now, establishes realistic goals, develops a balanced action plan, sustains attention to change, and monitors progress-the main steps necessary for achieving long-term success.

YOUR REVIEW

Dear Reader,

Let me seize this opportunity to express my deepest gratitude to each and every one of you for sparing your time to read my book, **"EVERY FUNDRAISER**: *Understanding the Courage to Ask and the Factors That Drive Financial Support.*" I am so grateful for your support, and I sincerely hope that the ideas and strategies shared in this book have inspired you in your fundraising activities.

Share Your Thoughts!

If you enjoyed the book, I'd love it if you could take a moment to leave a star review. Your review helps me both as an author to improve, and other readers to find the book. Here's how to leave a review:

1. Head to the store where you bought the book.
2. Find the review section.
3. Rate the book and leave a comment!

Whether it be a few words about what you learned or how the book inspired you, every review counts!

If you enjoyed **"EVERY FUNDRAISER,"** I invite you to explore my other books. Each is crafted with the same passion and dedication to the delivery of insight and useful advice as you have found here. Some of my other works you may want to consider:

- [**THE BOLD & BANKABLE FEMINIST**]
Amazon Book Link: https://www.amazon.com/dp/B0DNTM9QF1

- [**WOMEN'S WORLD OF MONEY**]
Amazon Book Link: https://www.amazon.com/dp/B0DNRC5G5F

- [**THE FINANCIAL ACTIVIST'S BLUEPRINT**]
Amazon Book Link: https://www.amazon.com/dp/B0DNWNRXSC

- [**FROM YOUR SHADOW**]
Amazon Book Link: https://www.amazon.com/dp/B0DP2Z1G2B

- [**THE HIDDEN BATTLE OF GIFTEDNESS**]
Amazon Book Link: https://www.amazon.com/dp/B0DPDN566N

- [**THE INNER WORLD OF CHILDREN**]
Amazon Book Link: https://www.amazon.com/dp/B0DP97Q3LN

- [**LENDING A HELPING HAND**]
Amazon Book Link: https://www.amazon.com/dp/B0DP7DKL17

- [**ESCAPING YOUR HEALTH KILLER**]
Amazon Book Link: https://www.amazon.com/dp/B0DPCGMD8G

- [**EVERY FUNDRAISER**]
Amazon Book Link: https://www.amazon.com/dp/B0DPPNRNHC

You can locate all my books by searching for Olojo Christiana on Amazon with the links above.

Your Support Is Important

Your review and recommendations are of great importance to me in growing my readership, and this will enable me to continue writing. Thank you once again for your support, and I look forward to hearing from you!

Best regards,

Olojo Christiana

ABOUT THE AUTHOR

Olojo Christiana is a health enthusiast, a wellness coach, and a writer who has dedicated her life to motivating and encouraging people to take responsibility for their health and live energetically. Having a background in nutrition and holistic health, Christiana combines evidence-based practices with personal experiences to inspire others on journeys toward well-being.

She, having struggled with her own health, has developed compassion for the weight many bear and translated that into action by providing them with practical tools and strategies to help overcome these issues. Christiana intends to build resilience, healthy habits, and continued growth through her writing, workshops, and coaching services.

Outside of writing or coaching, Christiana spends time in nature, being mindful, and connecting to the community. She deeply believes that every individual has the potential to break free from health killers and unleash a life of vitality and joy

9 798302 738400